Human Botany

Human Botany

Poems by

John Raffetto

Cover design by Shay Culligan

ISBN: 978-1-952326-26-4

Kelsay Books
502 South 1040 East, A-119
American Fork, Utah, 84003

for Kathy and Michael

In loving memory
of my parents John and Mary

Acknowledgments

Special thanks to all the editors for the following publications, where most of the poems in this book first appeared:

"Nostalgia & The Dead" in *Literary Orphans*

"Istanbul Spice Market" in *Poetry Quarterly*

"Chess is Life & Hawaiian Evolution" in *Exact Change Only*

"Sense of Place & Colorado Grassland" in *Gloom Cupboard*

"The Death of Edward Abbey" in *Word Catalyst*

"Cenote in Sian Ka'am" in *The Balloon*

"Trout River Newfoundland" in *Coldnoon*

"Museum of Insomnia & Jukebox Man" in *BlazeVOX*

"Chicago, The Full Moon, Last Visit to Nursing Home, The Letter & Liberace" in *Red Fez*

"Star Poet & Venezia" in *Wilderness House*

"It's Coming" in *Spank the Carp*

"Climate Change" in *UCity Review*

"Fury of Uncertain Memory" in *Ariel Chart*

"Botanical Insomnia" in *Picaroon Poetry*

"Photosynthesis (without equations)" in *Pangolin Review*

"The Yellow House" in *Angelic Dynamo*

"Divine" in *Adelaide Literary Magazine*

"Western Markers" nominated for Pushcart Prize 2017

"Mom's Last Ride" in *Magnolia Review*

"Fury of Uncertain Memory" is a cento of poets; Mary Oliver, Stuart Dybek, Linda Paten, Gary Snyder, Donald Hall, Sandra Cisneros, Charles Simic, Sharon Olds, Octavio Paz

In Appreciation

Special loving thanks to Kathy Bergen for her support and editing expertise.

In loving memory of my Uncle John Garvey, who shared his love of literature, introduced me to various writers and provided inspiration and support.

Thanks to Bill Yarrow for his thoughtful suggestions and ideas.

Thanks to all my friends and family for their encouragement of my poetry over the years.

Contents

Chapter 3

Chapter 1

if you don't know where you are you don't know who you are
—Wendell Berry

Sense of place is the sixth sense an eternal compass and map
made by memory and spatial perception together
—Rebecca Solnit

Sense of Place

Sonoran
volcanic light.
Anasazi ruins and dust
cover hollow eyes
of Apache warriors.

In the shadows, pale-lipped thieves fondle
temples and Mexican peasants.

Cattle rustlers watch cable television
on the banks of asphalt streams.
Metal roofs brace western railroad tracks
carrying Caribbean rum
on the spines of burnt field workers,
whose knotted hands hold nursing babies.

Tendril barbed-wire fence
frames a post card
for a Tucson gallery.

Carefully we approach the town from
a covered wagon given to us by
Geronimo's uncle,
who repaired his Cadillac
with sagebrush wrenches and whiskey fists.

All taverns are closed for Sabbath.
I bless the alkaline soil and dig
Cholla roots to place on a grave
of a slain cowboy
near the empty arroyo.

Colorado Grassland

Shallow prairie
of perfect silence
endures upon
worn plateaus
swept into burnt foothills.

Sagebrush and pale winds
flatten the void
of dry rain
and machines
lost in a
Pawnee ghost-dance.

Trout River Newfoundland

This western outpost
of sailors
and fishermen is
idle.
The salty cod have vanished
in greedy
waters.

Fishing shacks
maroon paint fades and
peels off
into the wind
near the Gulf of St. Lawrence.

Lobster traps and buoys
stacked neatly-
wait for another season.
A man with red calloused knuckles
slowly stretches a fishing net to dry,
stares at the man with a camera.

The cramped grocery store
displays frozen ham steaks
and canned vegetables,
along with bandages and tobacco.
Elderly men sit
near the door in wooden chairs
and observe all
saying nothing,
only a barely perceptible nod
as someone passes.

A man repairs a pick-up truck
in a battered aluminum garage,
turns to watch
someone who walks
on the muddy gravel road
near an idle lumber mill.

The majestic fjords draw tourists
who pass through town
quickly
and leave
with photographs.
The one-story school braces
for September
as children will soon gather,
later to flee
for jobs and city life.

All who remain
just sit.

Venezia

Empty moonlit piazza
grey cobblestone and
burnt sienna walls
on arched path.

Under a lone streetlamp
a solitary figure stands
suitcase in hand,
looks at me
offers no emotion
or quip,
near the narrow canal
a vacant boat is docked.

Vaporous opera
echoes from a window.
A white haired woman with
grey eyes
pierces the dark piazza
as the man with the suitcase
vanishes into jolted shadows.

Yes
I am here tonight
and the next day
staying in a weathered *pension*
where sensuous moans
emanate from the next room.
A reminder of
lost love—
as the scent
of espresso
warms the night.

Hawaiian Evolution

The island is a dream running backward
into the big bang.
Lava footprints glow
under a ringed moon—
spanning the ancient song
off thunderous waves
and hollowed cliffs—
carved
from white ginger.

Garfield Park Conservatory

Sunlight
under
symmetrical
glass panes,
wavelengths
between me and the galaxies
where slow growth
is the norm,
as seeds become trees
in real time
not
light years away.

Under glass
is warm,
insulated with chlorophyll
through my veins,
a cozy quilt
on snowy mornings
where I am veiled
behind a greenhouse door,
to the hissing of hot metal pipes.
as steam
settles on glass.

Under glass
shaded in July
sunlight
reflected away from
humid
terra cotta
pools,
slippery
sifted soil

dry to the touch,
as rare species
find a habitat
secure
from predators and disease.

Under glass
landscape art
on motionless display
of vibrant purples and crimson,
tropical leaves of netted veins
as spiky cycads
mirrored
on a waterfall.

Visitors explore
the conservatory
become unfettered,
content for a moment
observe palm roots and vanilla vines
on transparent leaves,
before returning to city traffic
and monkey mind.

Photosynthesis (without equations)

Photosynthesis reveals
a meditation
dreamscape of fossils,
a cosmic crawl
toward life force
past and present.

Photosynthesis reflects
a solar glow of
watery inhalation,
breathing dark matter,
a disjointed pigment
of a blue green ghost.

Photosynthesis offers
a folly
of burst molecules
electric in a swampy skin,
an ephemeral ocean
of death and decay.

Photosynthesis proclaims
a dazzled synthesis
of sugary
transfer,
an emerald glow
beyond
measured time,
the end and beginning,
an eternal web
that is the source
of all life.

Cenote in Sian Ka'am

Craters of sunken limestone
surround Mayan children
and tangled mangroves
where a jaguar lies
waiting for the final footstep
into the rainforests
of Guatemala.

A refugee washes dust from
a night bus ride
in a cenote.
Where the sky is born
and the earth breathes.

Istanbul Spice Market

Shoulder to shoulder,
a squeeze of tourists
as we pass under a stone arch
that spans centuries
and a cobblestone alley.

Cumin and saffron
sculptured
as mountains along
the Bosphorus,
separate a continent,
streetcars,
a cinnamon mosque.

Fabrics
glow
and paprika
leather jackets
sway
in weathered corridors of
dried roots and flowers.

Turmeric stains
refugees,
head covered women and
wide eyed tourists,
as fish glisten on ice
from the Black Sea,
shouts of vendors
hammer offers
to everyone
with
acts of jugglery
from the Tower of Babel.

Surrendering to a nearby cafe
that offers comfort—
an escape,
our shoulders
soothed
as we sip Turkish
sage tea
adrift on a
Babylonian sea.

The Death of Edward Abbey

Quiet
red dust morning
descends upon a sleeping coyote
near bright cactus and soft pinyon.
Rocks breathe into pure chalk bones
caging a pulsating heart.

A turkey vulture glides
as a clear desert wind pushes his wings north—
following music from an empty
adobe window,
awakening the coyote
who vanishes
into a dry river bed
abandoning the sun
to wander
alone.

Western Markers

bright sun
greyhound station across
main street cafe
grilled cheese
served on plastic plates

dust of narrow gauge tracks
black smoke inhales a solitary aspen grove
where a canyon's blue horizon
swallows pinyon air and empty beer cans
into the foothills of route 66
where dinosaur bones and buffalo skulls
peer into dry arroyos on cactus flats

alone in a distant motel
cold metal floors and rust
empty and lost
fog on chiseled pacific shore
damp emerald
covers an indigo sky
where frantic rent-a-car desks
and midnight coffee
wait
for late west bound train
leaving flagstaff pine scent

turquoise pottery along muddy
rio grande
sunset on a gravel road
a flat tire repaired with whisky
grease smeared wrench
pastel pueblos
vacant for centuries
now with air conditioned carpets

search stars for answers
or at least a phone number of someone in south dakota
friends embrace never to forget
the snow in a colorado canyon that healed
scars of a summer
train over sierra rivers and empty scotch bottles

colorado plateau evening
opens to reveal bones of zen stars

Chicago (history lesson)

Chicago is the flat prairie lake
wild onion breeze
slow canoe by
DuSable Indians and Anglo fools
paths of occasional bloody portage.

Wooden shacks
wooden mud
wooden swamp roads
a fine speck on eastern maps
where bankers strap gold
on beaver pelts.

A foggy betrayal
eyes crossed
deeds signed
in sandy saloons
the forged history lesson
a paper chase
through an epic sea.

Coal burns
lumber from Michigan woods
neatly stacked by the river
kindling
for a dry
October evening.

A bribe
a wink of an eye
a casual palm
greased by stockyard manure
a big shouldered exit
a sooty silhouette

under elevated tracks
where pigeons feast.

In your face city
distant from eastern disdain
laughs bughouse anarchists
billy-clubbed again and again
on fast trains toward the gallows.

A swim backwards
belly up to the gulf
a fishless glide.
As machine
gunned
politicians
dust Black Sox
runs and losses.

Chicago is the whitest of cities
and the darkest
always separate and unequal
streetcar tracks divide the
century—
death by knife
gun or rope
a jazz sunrise on the south side
stumbles into a bootleg
sunset.

A welcome
to Jim Crow refugees
with shadow freedom
amongst crowded factories
where streetcars drop passengers

going in different directions
gates locked for the night.

Sky art
clouds conceal masterpieces
without paint or easel
where the avant guarded their literati
in pickle alley.

Casting a long shadow
over beefy faces
tattooed opera and sips champagne
at galleries
that masquerade silk kittens.

Postwar flight
without tickets
or directions
coal stained apartments
remain as
construction
drains one by one
mesmerized by white lawns
and riots
what remains?

Redirection
resets
rearranges
bloody boundaries
panic peddles through
provincial neighborhoods
who remains?

Chicago is generations
of lake prairie wetlands
reclaims empty lots
as children
quietly
walk to school.

Climate Change

The perch in Lake Michigan
are using anti-depressants.
Don't forget the lonely Spotted Owl
addicted to Xanax
as they find shelter
in Pacific Coast pulpwood.
Then there is the howler monkey
who prefers natural St. John's wort
to soothe jangled nerves.

Yes the list is long.

The only way out is
out,
pushed from fragmented habitats,
an exodus
to a zoo
as human botany
observes
iphone in hand
a selfie
deleted
of natural history
a cry
in a mounted museum.

Chapter 2

it's strange how we hold on to pieces of the past
while we wait for our futures
— Ally Benaim

The past beats inside of me like a second heart
— John Banville

Chess is Life

Bobby Fischer became angry
when I mentioned Spassky
how he felt humiliated by Soviet women
hunger for an American checkmate.
My presence seems to torment him
as he pulled out a stiletto and
craved my wooden rook into sawdust.

Bobby kicked over the table
scattering chess pieces
like lost children.
But I refused to move
I ask again,
why Iceland?
He stared at me.
Speaking slowly
about the women.
The coastline.
The cold
War.

Nostalgia

Is nostalgia
the material and concrete
days before
a respite
an illusion or trickster coyote
lost in clouds and mist.

Is nostalgia
an anchor or heavy burden
a cry for help
the setting sun
locked into a
permanent horizon.

Is nostalgia
a rhythm of song
a cocked eye on
a twisted smile
a time before time
the beginning or end.

Is nostalgia
the hinge on the door
of perception
transcending lost souls
a solo bus ride into
a blizzard.

Is nostalgia
an island
a castle
a corner tavern
or a broken record
spinning off the turntable

the mighty cause defeated.

Is nostalgia
a past sun
calm between waves
the memory of a ghost train
jumping the tracks
a detour with
flashing lights.

Is nostalgia
an empty closet
once filled with jewels
a midnight mirage
of sleepless villages
torn by endless plagues.

Is nostalgia
what never was
a finger in the eye
blinding a shepherd
finding his lost flock.

Is nostalgia
really nostalgic
or a future
cosmic blast
that returns us
to the moment.

Liberace

Liberace was in the street
using a jackhammer
repairing a curb.
He was determined,
sweating.
His sequined suit was too warm
for a July afternoon
the jarring jackhammer
dislodged his purple boa
which matched his velvet pants.
He stopped to sip a sarsaparilla
wiping his brow.

People would stop
and ask him to play Clair de Lune.
He'd shake his head and continue
concrete dust settled
upon his leather shoes,
the endless sound of the jackhammer
filled the neighborhood.

After six hours
he finished,
walked away to applause
as loud as the jackhammer.
He smiled and waved to the crowd
as he strolled down an alley
disappearing into a house
and found a dark closet to rest in.

Star Poet

he can be called a star of poetry in America...
women also like the handsome poet
—taken from an online biography of Mark Strand

How do you do it?
I must ask him.
As I peer from the roof behind concrete gargoyles,
stumble behind thick oak trunks on the quad,
hiding between wooden pews of Rockefeller Chapel.
How do you do it?
To rouse women to unfasten their brassieres?

The women are lined up at Mandel Hall
he walks and one by one
another brassiere drops to the dark marble floor
all sizes and colors.

I must ask him
what works best
images,
contractions,
fewer adjectives,
which stirs the unfastening of brassieres?

The solitary Plaisance
suddenly swarms with women.
I push myself through the crowd,
approach carefully
and ask him about Prince Edward
where no man is an island.

He wanders by
oblivious
as mist drifts from his shoulders,
holding a mirror

41

that he lifts toward me as I ask,
how do you do it
to inspire women to unfasten their brassieres?

Jukebox Man

Seeburg jukebox
vertical records stacked
fragile as fine china
shoe polish black with
lollipop red Columbia label.

The heavy arm drops the needle on turntable
spinning 78 rpm
crackles
Billie Holiday smooth tormented voice
emerges
from vinyl grooves—
somewhere in a South Side tavern
patrons laugh loudly,
sip Old Granddad whisky
in Chesterfield haze—
the bartender nods to the man
with the brown fedora and
green metal tool box
removing dimes and nickels
from the jukebox—
replacing records from a cardboard box.
As he leaves the tavern
he hears a sudden crack outside
ricocheting into the night
but nothing like he heard
overseas during the war—

shrugging it away
goes to his 1951 Mercury
and drives to another service call.

Hopper

Edward Hopper was
a lonely grouch.
Painting solitary
streets
lighthouses
an occasional nude.

His fedora tight
on his head
his stern face
looks through you.

Yet his paintings
had
a clarity
a stillness
beyond shadows
or elevated trains
where the viewer
felt a familiar
loneliness
or a moment of freedom
in bright sunlight.

The Letter

I suggest to James Joyce
I'd mail the letter for him.
His eyesight poor,
glasses don't fit
his mind without focus
or logic
unable to accomplish Gaelic puzzles,
the riddle of existence
all a folly.

The letter is important
it speaks to all
Victorian publishers as
ships board for America
no one understands,
that Paris was my Dublin
and Dublin was my Paris
Trieste on the border
where Dos Passos
stumbled into socialism
a pun
spun
on the run.

Yes I tried to mail the letter
but didn't have the correct postage.

Joyce didn't seem to care,
as he tipped his hat to the mailbox
tapped his cane to the ground
streams into
fragmented
consciousness,
it's June 16th

and still
the letter not mailed.

The Yellow House

Worn shoes crunch the gravel street
as daytime flattens into starry nights.
Steel tracks hoist a steam engine past
black tile roofs bitten by sun
and dry winds of southern France.

Mixing colors in a tight blue bedroom
hallucination grooves and brush strokes
torn at midnight from echoes of laughter—
an escape from a blazing scythe
of Holland grain fields
swung with calloused hands and hungry eyes.

Swirling sun on a bloody afternoon
the vision is lost
slumped upon a wooden bed
in the blue bedroom
at the yellow house.

Chapter 3

insomnia has a romantic way of making the moon
feel like perfect company
                                        —Sabrina Benaim

Dying is a wild night and a new road
                                        —Emily Dickinson

Museum of Insomnia

2 am
Sleepless
again
lying motionless
eyes closed
mind soars
to my private night museum,
to wrestle
a lurking force
upon winding galleries
as hallways extend
beyond vaporous rooms
as blank faces
watch my
slumberous mirage
as a clock ticks.

2:30 am
A cacophony of silence
follows moonlight
as sleep misses the final exit
no one to hear the fury
and witness
an apparition of
grandfather spirit.

3 am
Time sputters
a Magritte silhouette
I recognize
floats past
yet don't recall,

elusive light offers hope
through musty shadows
a pornography of memories.

3:30 am
I converse with dead relatives
alpha and beta ghosts
who pace back and forth
eyelids never close
a rapid heartbeat
a shortness of breath
as vacant eyes of
gray faces
scold me good-bye.

4 am
Tears engulf childhood streets,
moonlight fog of
willowy figures who
disappear and reappear in
mirrored arcades,
barkers call the dead
who laugh a cold laugh
at insomniac dreams.

The Dead

The dead sometimes
are dying for years
buried at sea or in
a wooden coffin
or burned unrecognizably
ashes to ashes
at 800 degrees.

Undertakers smile at frozen years
as buzzards fly
among clouds' long corridor
ending abruptly
vanished in a short span.

A rocky boat follows the north star
only to succumb to toxic fumes or
a quick hand
a gun
a blade
politically poisoned
on a abandoned dirt road,
decapitated with a laugh
all cries silenced.

Please
please no children
snuffed out before introductions
a family of headstones
lined upright beyond the horizon
where the sun sets
golden orange
fading into shades of black.

The rattle comes slowly for some
mirrors under the nose
pennies on the eyes
fear of the last breath
while remembering
when times were good.

The Full Moon

All look at the full moon.
Old girlfriends
past teachers and guides.
Elderly souls with filmy eyes blink twice
before focusing.
Children laugh and hide from
the flat white face.
Young parents hold their children
and together sing into the night sky.
Prisoners do not look upward
why should they?
The dead would
if they could,
maybe spirits see more
than a full moon.
Speaking in voices that understand
why we all look at the full moon.

Last Visit at the Nursing Home

The shadows from clear white sun
are pale,
trees out of view
only a glimpse of changing skies.

With speckled hand
he scratches grey hair with
a slow movement from stiff limbs,
and turns to sleep.

A sterile room of plastic flowers,
vacant eyes
fade into endless television chatter
echoes in
urine corridors.

His laughter
silent
follows a painless
shallow breath
as he takes his final
stroll past pulsating headstones
of Spoon River
soon to be
sleeping on the hill.

Fury of Uncertain Memory

You lay in your last sleep
death is a memory of rivers with no names
a system of ghosts
open the curtains of your being
death passes us
the voice of the last cricket
a street whose name and number has been erased
before you became a cloud.

It's the metallic hour
night feels tight as a jar
watery night creatures
slam against each other
float above organ's rosy music
erratic complicated shape
fury of your memory
from loneliness I sleep
when will the night end?

I sat at the cold
applauding winds
excellence in a knife throw
the brain's shooting gallery.

I am on a parapet looking down
what are the habits of paradise
a crime of nostalgia
just wait a while
the water will run dear
tomorrow watches us all day.

Divine

A comedy?

Inferno

Dark fraudulent night
sleepless shadows
resonate gray masks
colorless voyage into circles of fury
no sunrise nor treacherous sunset
alone by the toxic river
only to return the next day.

Purgatorio

Bland hungry terrace
splashed face of proudly departed
a wrathful detour from humble madness
invisible to impassive crowds
a short breath
climbing
beleaguered from flight
only to return the next day.

Paradiso

Empty stars in night sky
a full moon
winds of hope
contemplate
the mystery
where knowledge wisely departs
planets evolve and expand
into the sweet abyss of days
only to return

to mystery
the next day.

Botanical Insomnia

Again I rewind the tape
looping endless
babble dreams
under
cycad moon.
Years spent in therapeutic
echo chambers
shadows of volcanic
palm
fronds
against gnarled oak branches—
a slow drip
of desired rest
cast aside
near streetlamp glow
the forgotten
and forgiven
lie in state
of green fossils
as the tape
sputters into a taut
endgame
as dawn approaches
through filtered
blinds.

Mom's Last Ride

The urn was cobalt blue
heavy for someone
who was skinny
in her youth.
Her ashes sat next to me
as she did many times
when I was a child riding the bus or el
or later in life as we rode to the grocery store.

This July morning
on the way to the cemetery
I played her favorite singer Nat King Cole
in the too low convertible
she never got to ride in.

At the cemetery
I approach a familiar plot.
They're all here now,
my mom the last to arrive
just like at the Christmas dinner table.

It's Coming

You know it's coming
a rattled breath
an unexpected fate
accosted you
or a loved one.

You hope it's not soon
or maybe never happens
but dust to dust
suffer into the grave night,
sitting at a wake
or *shiva*
pacing the carpet,
glance at the clock.

You fear the fear
where there is no hope
reflect on past love
and marvel at
those glorious days
when there was
no time
or need to ponder
loss
of this
brilliant morning.

About the Author

John Raffetto is a lifelong resident of Chicago. Some of his poetry has been published in print and online magazines such as *Gloom Cupboard, Wilderness House, BlazeVox, Literary Orphans, Poetry Quarterly & Exact Change.* One of his poems was nominated for a Pushcart Prize in 2017. He holds degrees from the University of Illinois and Northeastern Illinois University and worked as a horticulturist and landscape designer for many years at the Chicago Park District. Its conservatories and parks were rich sources of inspiration for poems concerning nature, people, and the city. Currently, He teaches courses at Newberry Library and Chicago Botanic Garden and has taught at local community colleges and museums. He lives with his wife, and they have an adult son.

www.ingramcontent.com/pod-product-compliance
Lightning Source LLC
Chambersburg PA
CBHW031152090426
42738CB00008B/1303